It's In My Hands

An Empowerment Journal for
the Journey to Total Well-Being

Alnita Trawick McClure

Copyright © 2009 Alnita Trawick McClure
All rights reserved.

ISBN: 1-4392-0755-0
ISBN-13: 9781439207550

Visit www.booksurge.com to order additional copies.

No part of this publication may be reproduced, stored in a retrieval system, or transmitted in any form or by any means – electronic, mechanical, photocopy, recording, scanning (except for quotations in reviews or articles) without prior written permission of the author.

Information in this journal is intended to motivate, inspire and empower.

> **BE A GOOD ANCESTOR. STAND FOR SOMETHING BIGGER THAN YOURSELF. ADD VALUE TO THE EARTH DURING YOUR SOJOURN.**

Excerpt taken from
Marian Wright Edelman's
Twenty-Five Lessons for Life Lanterns; A Memoir of Mentors

This journal honors the legacy of achievement and service left by my grandparents, Dock and Lecie Mitchell Trawick.

I am grateful to my parents, Mason Attucks Trawick and Gracie Simpson Trawick, for my heritage of empowering values.

ACKNOWLEDGMENTS

Creating this journal has strengthened my belief in the value of significant relationships in my life. They provided the clarity, focus and encouragement that I needed to bring this project to completion.

I am grateful

> To Gwendolyn Moore and Phyllis Jones who understood and supported my vision from the beginning.

> To Elois Saucer who understands my journey and provides sound counsel as I travel it.

> To the women in the 2005 Experiencing God Bible Study Group of the Journey Christian Church for nourishing my spirit.

> To the women in Memphis, Tennessee; Raleigh/Durham, North Carolina; Phoenix, Arizona; and Oak Harbor, Washington who participated in focus groups and candidly expressed their feelings about their empowerment.

> To Denise Alexander for her thoughtful critique of the first journal draft.

> To my new friend, Nina Brock, who immediately understood my need to create a journal that represents a spiritual mindset.

> To Natalie Bullock Brown who has taught me that one can benefit from the wisdom of younger, spiritually centered women.

> To Janice Taff, Mary Hughes and Sheila Williams for their graphics and printing support.

I cherish the treasure I have found in all of these women!

I am especially grateful to my husband, Dr. Jesse F. McClure, who always challenges me to "stretch" and "think big" and to my children, Tasha C. McClure and Jesse F. McClure III (Katie), whose unconditional love and support are always present.

> IT'S IN MY HANDS IS A STATEMENT I HAVE USED IN MANY SPEECHES. THE STATEMENT IS POWERFUL AND THIS JOURNAL ALLOWS ALL TO TAKE THE STATEMENT TO A HIGHER LEVEL. "TOTAL WELL-BEING" ENCOMPASSES ALL OF "ME" AND "YOU".

Henrietta Augustus Harris, Ed.D.
Dean of Student Performance, Dillard University
New Orleans, Louisiana

FOREWORD

It is refreshing to find an empowerment tool for women of all ages. It affords us the opportunity to examine our inner spirits and commit to using what we already possess to empower ourselves on our journeys toward total well-being. *It's In My Hands* persuades women to examine ingrained patterns, through introspection, to discover what works, to discard what does not, and to develop a vision of total well-being.

Women who take this journey will define and live their unique total well-being.

Knowing true well-being empowers women to strive for a life of fulfillment and total wellness. *It's In My Hands* will assist women in developing an intentional action plan for their lives that focuses their attention to the mind, body and spirit.

A deliberate focus on our inner strengths as we imagine healthy and fulfilled lives coupled with a written plan for commitment to feed the mind, body and spirit will yield an empowered life, inner peace and joy.

This journal is reflective of Alnita Trawick McClure's years of concern for and commitment to maximizing the potential of women's inner and outward expressions of empowerment. It is with gratitude to her that I am encouraged to do what I want and need to do to live my best life each day on my journey to total well-being.

Elois Wyche Saucer
Decatur, Georgia

INTRODUCTION

IT'S IN YOUR HANDS: your greatest potential for a prosperous, healthy, successful, significant, contented and happy life. It is your total well-being, unique to you and defined only by you. It is you at your best!

Your journey to total well-being does not begin "when" or "if" something happens; it begins NOW with a vision of your total well-being:

> Significant relationships—family, social, professional and spiritual.

> What you want out of life.

> The impact you want to have on your family, your community, institutions and the world.

> Your state of prosperity and abundance.

> Your mental and physical health.

> Your legacy, your mark on the world.

This journal is a tool to guide and motivate you to empower yourself by actively engaging your mind, body and spirit on your journey.

The Journal

Defines total well-being:

- Empowers you to act on the belief that you are responsible, accountable and remarkable.

- Gives examples of ways to engage and fuel your mind, body and spirit to live your vision of total well-being.

- Puts you in charge of your journey. You define, record, embrace and act on your vision of total well-being.

- Encourages you to conduct an accountability check halfway through the journal by reflecting on how far you have traveled. Page 85

- Provides an opportunity to recommit to and expand your vision of total well-being. Page 137

- Reminds you on each page to focus on the wholeness of mind, body and spirit.

- Challenges you to tell the story of your journey to total well-being, to become an example of total well-being and to invest in the well-being of others. Page 138 and 139

- Gives you an opportunity to meet the author. Page 141

It's In Your Hands!
This is the time to begin your journey to
Total Well-Being!

MY JOURNEY TO TOTAL WELL-BEING

Total Well-Being offers the greatest potential for a prosperous, healthy, successful, significant, contented and happy life. It is …

Me *at my best.*

My *destiny.*

My *purpose.*

My *uniqueness.*

> **EMPOWER YOURSELF: BE ACCOUNTABLE AND RESPONSIBLE FOR YOUR TOTAL WELL-BEING.**

THIS JOURNAL IS MY PASSAGE TO TOTAL WELL-BEING.

This passage is my belief that ...

I *am responsible and accountable for my choices in life.*

There *is greatness in me.*

What *I think controls my behavior and affects how individuals and the world respond to me.*

It *is never too late to define or redefine myself and take the path to total well-being.*

WHAT IS YOUR VISION OF YOUR TOTAL WELL-BEING?

DESCRIBE YOURSELF AT YOUR BEST.
(Review Pages 11 and 13)

IT'S IN MY HANDS

MY VISION OF MY TOTAL WELL-BEING...

I imagine it, I define it, I picture it and I embrace it.

Halfway through my journey, I will pause, reflect and celebrate the actions I have taken to live my vision of total well-being.

(See page 85)

IT'S IN MY HANDS

I LIVE MY VISION ...

I *am empowered everyday to take responsibility for my total well-being by actively focusing on engaging my mind, body and spirit.*

WAYS I EXPAND MY MIND

MY MIND

KNOWLEDGE AND SKILLS: *Continuous learning through reading, taking part in discussion groups, workshops, and conferences.*

NEW IDEAS: *Moving beyond my comfort zone; contact with knowledgeable and successful people.*

POSITIVE THOUGHTS: *Imagining life's greatest possibilities.*

DISCIPLINE AND PERSISTENCE: *Living an organized and focused life regardless of obstacles, disappointments and failures; upholding a "can do" attitude.*

CHOICES*: Making decisions that support my goals and total well-being.*

SELF CONFIDENCE: *Developing awareness of and using my talents, skills and strengths.*

> **MY BODY IS A TEMPLE: I HONOR, RESPECT AND CARE FOR IT.**

MY BODY

POSITIVE IMAGE: *Striving toward my best physical appearance and mental state.*

HEALTH STATUS: *Knowing how mentally and physically healthy I am.*

HEALTH CARE: *Finding a primary health care provider who promotes healthy living, focuses on illness prevention and delivers quality medical care.*

LIFESTYLE: *Taking responsibility for my health by knowing my health risks and engaging in practices that promote mental and physical health and prevent illness, such* *as proper nutrition, exercise and health screenings.*

HONOR: *Reserving time for rest, relaxation, pleasure and pampering.*

RESPECT: *Abstaining from the use, abuse and exposure to legal and illegal substances such as alcohol, drugs and tobacco.*

> **MY SPIRIT IS THE ESSENCE OF WHO I AM: I NOURISH IT.**

MY SPIRIT

PRAYER, MEDITATION, BIBLE STUDY AND REFLECTION: *Dedicating time to connect to a higher power.*

A CALM AND PEACEFUL ENVIRONMENT: *Replacing chaos and clutter with order and discipline.*

SPIRITUAL GROWTH: *Reading and listening to inspirational media (periodicals, radio, television, tapes, CDs), joining in religious activities, surrounding myself with positive people.*

SERVICE: *Using my time, talents and assets to improve the lives of others and the community.*

***EMPATHY AND SYMPATHY:** Understanding the pain, suffering and circumstances of others.*

***AUTHENTICITY:** Knowing and loving my true self.*

***GRATITUDE:** Meditating and expressing thanks daily.*

***RELEASE OF THE PAST:** Letting go of hurts, disappointments, fears and failures.*

***POSITIVE RELATIONSHIPS:** Connecting and interacting with family, friends and networks that inspire, encourage, energize and bring out the best in me.*

***A**ctively engaging my MIND, BODY and SPIRIT propels me to total well-being.*

***M**y Personal inspirational and encouraging thoughts that support my journey...*

Date: _____

EACH DAY OFFERS A NEW OPPORTUNITY TO LIVE MY VISION OF TOTAL WELL-BEING.

❑ MY MIND

❑ MY BODY

❑ MY SPIRIT

Date: _____

EACH DAY OFFERS A NEW OPPORTUNITY TO LIVE MY VISION OF TOTAL WELL-BEING.

❑ MY MIND

❑ MY BODY

❑ MY SPIRIT

Date: _____

EACH DAY OFFERS A NEW OPPORTUNITY TO LIVE MY VISION OF TOTAL WELL-BEING.

❑ MY MIND

❑ MY BODY

❑ MY SPIRIT

Date: _____

EACH DAY OFFERS A NEW OPPORTUNITY TO LIVE MY VISION OF TOTAL WELL-BEING.

❑ MY MIND

❑ MY BODY

❑ MY SPIRIT

Date: _____

EACH DAY OFFERS A NEW OPPORTUNITY TO LIVE MY VISION OF TOTAL WELL-BEING.

❑ MY MIND

❑ MY BODY

❑ MY SPIRIT

Date: _____

EACH DAY OFFERS A NEW OPPORTUNITY TO LIVE MY VISION OF TOTAL WELL-BEING.

❑ MY MIND

❑ MY BODY

❑ MY SPIRIT

Date: _____

EACH DAY OFFERS A NEW OPPORTUNITY TO LIVE MY VISION OF TOTAL WELL-BEING.

❏ MY MIND

❏ MY BODY

❏ MY SPIRIT

Date: _____

EACH DAY OFFERS A NEW OPPORTUNITY TO LIVE MY VISION OF TOTAL WELL-BEING.

❑ MY MIND

❑ MY BODY

❑ MY SPIRIT

Date: _____

EACH DAY OFFERS A NEW OPPORTUNITY TO LIVE MY VISION OF TOTAL WELL-BEING.

❑ MY MIND

❑ MY BODY

❑ MY SPIRIT

Date: _____

EACH DAY OFFERS A NEW OPPORTUNITY TO LIVE MY VISION OF TOTAL WELL-BEING.

❏ MY MIND

❏ MY BODY

❏ MY SPIRIT

Date: _____

EACH DAY OFFERS A NEW OPPORTUNITY TO LIVE MY VISION OF TOTAL WELL-BEING.

❑ MY MIND

❑ MY BODY

❑ MY SPIRIT

Date: _____

EACH DAY OFFERS A NEW OPPORTUNITY TO LIVE MY VISION OF TOTAL WELL-BEING.

❑ MY MIND

❑ MY BODY

❑ MY SPIRIT

Date: _____

EACH DAY OFFERS A NEW OPPORTUNITY TO LIVE MY VISION OF TOTAL WELL-BEING.

❑ MY MIND

❑ MY BODY

❑ MY SPIRIT

Date: _____

EACH DAY OFFERS A NEW OPPORTUNITY TO LIVE MY VISION OF TOTAL WELL-BEING.

❑ MY MIND

❑ MY BODY

❑ MY SPIRIT

Date: _____

EACH DAY OFFERS A NEW OPPORTUNITY TO LIVE MY VISION OF TOTAL WELL-BEING.

❏ MY MIND

❏ MY BODY

❏ MY SPIRIT

Date: _____

EACH DAY OFFERS A NEW OPPORTUNITY TO LIVE MY VISION OF TOTAL WELL-BEING.

❑ MY MIND

❑ MY BODY

❑ MY SPIRIT

Date: _____

EACH DAY OFFERS A NEW OPPORTUNITY TO LIVE MY VISION OF TOTAL WELL-BEING.

❏ MY MIND

❏ MY BODY

❏ MY SPIRIT

Date: _____

EACH DAY OFFERS A NEW OPPORTUNITY TO LIVE MY VISION OF TOTAL WELL-BEING.

❏ MY MIND

❏ MY BODY

❏ MY SPIRIT

Date: _____

EACH DAY OFFERS A NEW OPPORTUNITY TO LIVE MY VISION OF TOTAL WELL-BEING.

❑ MY MIND

❑ MY BODY

❑ MY SPIRIT

Date: _____

EACH DAY OFFERS A NEW OPPORTUNITY TO LIVE MY VISION OF TOTAL WELL-BEING.

❑ MY MIND

❑ MY BODY

❑ MY SPIRIT

Date: _____

EACH DAY OFFERS A NEW OPPORTUNITY TO LIVE MY VISION OF TOTAL WELL-BEING.

❏ MY MIND

❏ MY BODY

❏ MY SPIRIT

Date: _____

EACH DAY OFFERS A NEW OPPORTUNITY TO LIVE MY VISION OF TOTAL WELL-BEING.

❏ MY MIND

❏ MY BODY

❏ MY SPIRIT

Date: _____

EACH DAY OFFERS A NEW OPPORTUNITY TO LIVE MY VISION OF TOTAL WELL-BEING.

❑ MY MIND

❑ MY BODY

❑ MY SPIRIT

Date: _____

EACH DAY OFFERS A NEW OPPORTUNITY TO LIVE MY VISION OF TOTAL WELL-BEING.

❏ MY MIND

❏ MY BODY

❏ MY SPIRIT

Date: _____

EACH DAY OFFERS A NEW OPPORTUNITY TO LIVE MY VISION OF TOTAL WELL-BEING.

❑ MY MIND

❑ MY BODY

❑ MY SPIRIT

Date: _____

EACH DAY OFFERS A NEW OPPORTUNITY TO LIVE MY VISION OF TOTAL WELL-BEING.

❑ MY MIND

❑ MY BODY

❑ MY SPIRIT

Date: _____

EACH DAY OFFERS A NEW OPPORTUNITY TO LIVE MY VISION OF TOTAL WELL-BEING.

❑ MY MIND

❑ MY BODY

❑ MY SPIRIT

Date: _____

EACH DAY OFFERS A NEW OPPORTUNITY TO LIVE MY VISION OF TOTAL WELL-BEING.

❑ MY MIND

❑ MY BODY

❑ MY SPIRIT

Date: _____

EACH DAY OFFERS A NEW OPPORTUNITY TO LIVE MY VISION OF TOTAL WELL-BEING.

❑ MY MIND

❑ MY BODY

❑ MY SPIRIT

Date: _____

EACH DAY OFFERS A NEW OPPORTUNITY TO LIVE MY VISION OF TOTAL WELL-BEING.

❑ MY MIND

❑ MY BODY

❑ MY SPIRIT

Date: _____

EACH DAY OFFERS A NEW OPPORTUNITY TO LIVE MY VISION OF TOTAL WELL-BEING.

❑ MY MIND

❑ MY BODY

❑ MY SPIRIT

Date: _____

EACH DAY OFFERS A NEW OPPORTUNITY TO LIVE MY VISION OF TOTAL WELL-BEING.

❑ MY MIND

❑ MY BODY

❑ MY SPIRIT

Date: _____

EACH DAY OFFERS A NEW OPPORTUNITY TO LIVE MY VISION OF TOTAL WELL-BEING.

❏ MY MIND

❏ MY BODY

❏ MY SPIRIT

Date: _____

EACH DAY OFFERS A NEW OPPORTUNITY TO LIVE MY VISION OF TOTAL WELL-BEING.

❑ MY MIND

❑ MY BODY

❑ MY SPIRIT

Date: _____

EACH DAY OFFERS A NEW OPPORTUNITY TO LIVE MY VISION OF TOTAL WELL-BEING.

❏ MY MIND

❏ MY BODY

❏ MY SPIRIT

Date: _____

EACH DAY OFFERS A NEW OPPORTUNITY TO LIVE MY VISION OF TOTAL WELL-BEING.

❑ MY MIND

❑ MY BODY

❑ MY SPIRIT

Date: _____

EACH DAY OFFERS A NEW OPPORTUNITY TO LIVE MY VISION OF TOTAL WELL-BEING.

❑ MY MIND

❑ MY BODY

❑ MY SPIRIT

Date: _____

EACH DAY OFFERS A NEW OPPORTUNITY TO LIVE MY VISION OF TOTAL WELL-BEING.

❑ MY MIND

❑ MY BODY

❑ MY SPIRIT

Date: _____

EACH DAY OFFERS A NEW OPPORTUNITY TO LIVE MY VISION OF TOTAL WELL-BEING.

❑ MY MIND

❑ MY BODY

❑ MY SPIRIT

Date: _____

EACH DAY OFFERS A NEW OPPORTUNITY TO LIVE MY VISION OF TOTAL WELL-BEING.

❏ MY MIND

❏ MY BODY

❏ MY SPIRIT

Date: _____

EACH DAY OFFERS A NEW OPPORTUNITY TO LIVE MY VISION OF TOTAL WELL-BEING.

❑ MY MIND

❑ MY BODY

❑ MY SPIRIT

Date: _____

EACH DAY OFFERS A NEW OPPORTUNITY TO LIVE MY VISION OF TOTAL WELL-BEING.

❑ MY MIND

❑ MY BODY

❑ MY SPIRIT

Date: _____

EACH DAY OFFERS A NEW OPPORTUNITY TO LIVE MY VISION OF TOTAL WELL-BEING.

❑ MY MIND

❑ MY BODY

❑ MY SPIRIT

Date: _____

EACH DAY OFFERS A NEW OPPORTUNITY TO LIVE MY VISION OF TOTAL WELL-BEING.

❑ MY MIND

❑ MY BODY

❑ MY SPIRIT

Date: _____

EACH DAY OFFERS A NEW OPPORTUNITY TO LIVE MY VISION OF TOTAL WELL-BEING.

❑ MY MIND

❑ MY BODY

❑ MY SPIRIT

Date: _____

EACH DAY OFFERS A NEW OPPORTUNITY TO LIVE MY VISION OF TOTAL WELL-BEING.

❑ MY MIND

❑ MY BODY

❑ MY SPIRIT

Date: _____

EACH DAY OFFERS A NEW OPPORTUNITY TO LIVE MY VISION OF TOTAL WELL-BEING.

❑ MY MIND

❑ MY BODY

❑ MY SPIRIT

IT'S IN MY HANDS

Date: _____

EACH DAY OFFERS A NEW OPPORTUNITY TO LIVE MY VISION OF TOTAL WELL-BEING.

❑ MY MIND

❑ MY BODY

❑ MY SPIRIT

Date: _____

EACH DAY OFFERS A NEW OPPORTUNITY TO LIVE MY VISION OF TOTAL WELL-BEING.

❏ MY MIND

❏ MY BODY

❏ MY SPIRIT

REFLECTION AND CELEBRATION

I have taken responsibility for my total well-being by actively engaging my mind, body and spirit.

I have expanded my mind, changed my thoughts and increased my skills by…

I have honored my body by…

I have nourished my spirit by…

Date: _____

EACH DAY OFFERS A NEW OPPORTUNITY TO LIVE MY VISION OF TOTAL WELL-BEING.

❑ MY MIND

❑ MY BODY

❑ MY SPIRIT

Date: _____

EACH DAY OFFERS A NEW OPPORTUNITY TO LIVE MY VISION OF TOTAL WELL-BEING.

❑ MY MIND

❑ MY BODY

❑ MY SPIRIT

Date: _____

EACH DAY OFFERS A NEW OPPORTUNITY TO LIVE MY VISION OF TOTAL WELL-BEING.

❏ MY MIND

❏ MY BODY

❏ MY SPIRIT

Date: _____

EACH DAY OFFERS A NEW OPPORTUNITY TO LIVE MY VISION OF TOTAL WELL-BEING.

❑ MY MIND

❑ MY BODY

❑ MY SPIRIT

Date: _____

EACH DAY OFFERS A NEW OPPORTUNITY TO LIVE MY VISION OF TOTAL WELL-BEING.

❑ MY MIND

❑ MY BODY

❑ MY SPIRIT

Date: _____

EACH DAY OFFERS A NEW OPPORTUNITY TO LIVE MY VISION OF TOTAL WELL-BEING.

❑ MY MIND

❑ MY BODY

❑ MY SPIRIT

Date: _____

EACH DAY OFFERS A NEW OPPORTUNITY TO LIVE MY VISION OF TOTAL WELL-BEING.

❑ MY MIND

❑ MY BODY

❑ MY SPIRIT

Date: _____

EACH DAY OFFERS A NEW OPPORTUNITY TO LIVE MY VISION OF TOTAL WELL-BEING.

❑ MY MIND

❑ MY BODY

❑ MY SPIRIT

Date: _____

EACH DAY OFFERS A NEW OPPORTUNITY TO LIVE MY VISION OF TOTAL WELL-BEING.

❑ MY MIND

❑ MY BODY

❑ MY SPIRIT

Date: _____

EACH DAY OFFERS A NEW OPPORTUNITY TO LIVE MY VISION OF TOTAL WELL-BEING.

❏ MY MIND

❏ MY BODY

❏ MY SPIRIT

Date: _____

EACH DAY OFFERS A NEW OPPORTUNITY TO LIVE MY VISION OF TOTAL WELL-BEING.

❑ MY MIND

❑ MY BODY

❑ MY SPIRIT

Date: _____

EACH DAY OFFERS A NEW OPPORTUNITY TO LIVE MY VISION OF TOTAL WELL-BEING.

❑ MY MIND

❑ MY BODY

❑ MY SPIRIT

Date: _____

EACH DAY OFFERS A NEW OPPORTUNITY TO LIVE MY VISION OF TOTAL WELL-BEING.

❑ MY MIND

❑ MY BODY

❑ MY SPIRIT

Date: _____

EACH DAY OFFERS A NEW OPPORTUNITY TO LIVE MY VISION OF TOTAL WELL-BEING.

❏ MY MIND

❏ MY BODY

❏ MY SPIRIT

Date: _____

EACH DAY OFFERS A NEW OPPORTUNITY TO LIVE MY VISION OF TOTAL WELL-BEING.

❑   MY MIND

❑   MY BODY

❑   MY SPIRIT

Date: _____

EACH DAY OFFERS A NEW OPPORTUNITY TO LIVE MY VISION OF TOTAL WELL-BEING.

❑ MY MIND

❑ MY BODY

❑ MY SPIRIT

Date: _____

EACH DAY OFFERS A NEW OPPORTUNITY TO LIVE MY VISION OF TOTAL WELL-BEING.

❏ MY MIND

❏ MY BODY

❏ MY SPIRIT

Date: _____

EACH DAY OFFERS A NEW OPPORTUNITY TO LIVE MY VISION OF TOTAL WELL-BEING.

❑ MY MIND

❑ MY BODY

❑ MY SPIRIT

Date: _____

EACH DAY OFFERS A NEW OPPORTUNITY TO LIVE MY VISION OF TOTAL WELL-BEING.

❑ MY MIND

❑ MY BODY

❑ MY SPIRIT

Date: _____

EACH DAY OFFERS A NEW OPPORTUNITY TO LIVE MY VISION OF TOTAL WELL-BEING.

❑ MY MIND

❑ MY BODY

❑ MY SPIRIT

Date: _____

EACH DAY OFFERS A NEW OPPORTUNITY TO LIVE MY VISION OF TOTAL WELL-BEING.

❑ MY MIND

❑ MY BODY

❑ MY SPIRIT

Date: _____

EACH DAY OFFERS A NEW OPPORTUNITY TO LIVE MY VISION OF TOTAL WELL-BEING.

❑ MY MIND

❑ MY BODY

❑ MY SPIRIT

Date: _____

EACH DAY OFFERS A NEW OPPORTUNITY TO LIVE MY VISION OF TOTAL WELL-BEING.

❑ MY MIND

❑ MY BODY

❑ MY SPIRIT

Date: _____

EACH DAY OFFERS A NEW OPPORTUNITY TO LIVE MY VISION OF TOTAL WELL-BEING.

❑ MY MIND

❑ MY BODY

❑ MY SPIRIT

Date: _____

EACH DAY OFFERS A NEW OPPORTUNITY TO LIVE MY VISION OF TOTAL WELL-BEING.

❏ MY MIND

❏ MY BODY

❏ MY SPIRIT

Date: _____

EACH DAY OFFERS A NEW OPPORTUNITY TO LIVE MY VISION OF TOTAL WELL-BEING.

❑ MY MIND

❑ MY BODY

❑ MY SPIRIT

Date: _____

EACH DAY OFFERS A NEW OPPORTUNITY TO LIVE MY VISION OF TOTAL WELL-BEING.

❑ MY MIND

❑ MY BODY

❑ MY SPIRIT

Date: _____

EACH DAY OFFERS A NEW OPPORTUNITY TO LIVE MY VISION OF TOTAL WELL-BEING.

❑ MY MIND

❑ MY BODY

❑ MY SPIRIT

Date: _____

EACH DAY OFFERS A NEW OPPORTUNITY TO LIVE MY VISION OF TOTAL WELL-BEING.

❑ MY MIND

❑ MY BODY

❑ MY SPIRIT

Date: _____

EACH DAY OFFERS A NEW OPPORTUNITY TO LIVE MY VISION OF TOTAL WELL-BEING.

❑ MY MIND

❑ MY BODY

❑ MY SPIRIT

Date: _____

EACH DAY OFFERS A NEW OPPORTUNITY TO LIVE MY VISION OF TOTAL WELL-BEING.

❏ MY MIND

❏ MY BODY

❏ MY SPIRIT

Date: _____

EACH DAY OFFERS A NEW OPPORTUNITY TO LIVE MY VISION OF TOTAL WELL-BEING.

❑ MY MIND

❑ MY BODY

❑ MY SPIRIT

Date: _____

EACH DAY OFFERS A NEW OPPORTUNITY TO LIVE MY VISION OF TOTAL WELL-BEING.

❏ MY MIND

❏ MY BODY

❏ MY SPIRIT

Date: _____

EACH DAY OFFERS A NEW OPPORTUNITY TO LIVE MY VISION OF TOTAL WELL-BEING.

❏ MY MIND

❏ MY BODY

❏ MY SPIRIT

Date: _____

EACH DAY OFFERS A NEW OPPORTUNITY TO LIVE MY VISION OF TOTAL WELL-BEING.

❑ MY MIND

❑ MY BODY

❑ MY SPIRIT

Date: _____

EACH DAY OFFERS A NEW OPPORTUNITY TO LIVE MY VISION OF TOTAL WELL-BEING.

❑ MY MIND

❑ MY BODY

❑ MY SPIRIT

Date: _____

EACH DAY OFFERS A NEW OPPORTUNITY TO LIVE MY VISION OF TOTAL WELL-BEING.

❑ MY MIND

❑ MY BODY

❑ MY SPIRIT

Date: _____

EACH DAY OFFERS A NEW OPPORTUNITY TO LIVE MY VISION OF TOTAL WELL-BEING.

☐ MY MIND

☐ MY BODY

☐ MY SPIRIT

Date: _____

EACH DAY OFFERS A NEW OPPORTUNITY TO LIVE MY VISION OF TOTAL WELL-BEING.

❑ MY MIND

❑ MY BODY

❑ MY SPIRIT

Date: _____

EACH DAY OFFERS A NEW OPPORTUNITY TO LIVE MY VISION OF TOTAL WELL-BEING.

❑ MY MIND

❑ MY BODY

❑ MY SPIRIT

Date: _____

EACH DAY OFFERS A NEW OPPORTUNITY TO LIVE MY VISION OF TOTAL WELL-BEING.

❑ MY MIND

❑ MY BODY

❑ MY SPIRIT

Date: _____

EACH DAY OFFERS A NEW OPPORTUNITY TO LIVE MY VISION OF TOTAL WELL-BEING.

❑ MY MIND

❑ MY BODY

❑ MY SPIRIT

Date: _____

EACH DAY OFFERS A NEW OPPORTUNITY TO LIVE MY VISION OF TOTAL WELL-BEING.

❏ MY MIND

❏ MY BODY

❏ MY SPIRIT

Date: _____

EACH DAY OFFERS A NEW OPPORTUNITY TO LIVE MY VISION OF TOTAL WELL-BEING.

❑ MY MIND

❑ MY BODY

❑ MY SPIRIT

Date: _____

EACH DAY OFFERS A NEW OPPORTUNITY TO LIVE MY VISION OF TOTAL WELL-BEING.

❑ MY MIND

❑ MY BODY

❑ MY SPIRIT

Date: _____

EACH DAY OFFERS A NEW OPPORTUNITY TO LIVE MY VISION OF TOTAL WELL-BEING.

❏ MY MIND

❏ MY BODY

❏ MY SPIRIT

Date: _____

EACH DAY OFFERS A NEW OPPORTUNITY TO LIVE MY VISION OF TOTAL WELL-BEING.

❑ MY MIND

❑ MY BODY

❑ MY SPIRIT

Date: _____

EACH DAY OFFERS A NEW OPPORTUNITY TO LIVE MY VISION OF TOTAL WELL-BEING.

❑ MY MIND

❑ MY BODY

❑ MY SPIRIT

Date: _____

EACH DAY OFFERS A NEW OPPORTUNITY TO LIVE MY VISION OF TOTAL WELL-BEING.

❑ MY MIND

❑ MY BODY

❑ MY SPIRIT

YOU HAVE TRAVELED A GREAT DISTANCE. AS YOU HAVE GROWN, YOUR POTENTIAL FOR GREATNESS HAS INCREASED. EXPAND YOUR VISION OF TOTAL WELL-BEING AND WRITE A NEW VISION STATEMENT.

… WELL-BEING BY …

I RECOMMIT TO MY VISION OF TOTAL WELL-BEING BY…

> **TELL YOUR STORY OF TOTAL WELL-BEING, BECOME AN EXAMPLE OF TOTAL WELL-BEING AND INVEST IN THE WELL-BEING OF OTHERS.**

A CHALLENGE

Don't Stop Now! Start Something!

Start a new chapter of your life—expand your horizon.

Start a group.

Join a group.

Start a family conversation about **total** well-being.

Develop and give a presentation about your journey.

Lead by example: mentor someone, become a spiritual mother, sister or volunteer.

"If you want to lift yourself up, lift up someone else."

– Booker T. Washington

ABOUT THE AUTHOR

Alnita Trawick McClure is president of CPR Strategies LLC, a consulting firm that aids organizations in developing social-marketing campaigns, messages and initiatives to improve the health and welfare of their target populations. CPR Strategies brings life to organizations.

Her career includes executive-level positions with health and human service systems in Memphis, Tennessee; Phoenix, Arizona; and the State of California. She received many honors and awards while serving in these positions. The Tennessee Hospital Association awarded Ms. McClure its Meritorious Service Award for transforming Mid-South Family Health Care Centers, Inc. into an innovative and financially stable corporation. Under her leadership, Mid-South also received recognition for its commitment to improving the health of the community through creative partnerships with neighborhood organizations, local corporations and governmental agencies.

During her tenure as Human Services Administrator for the City of Phoenix Arizona, she created a program designed to move parenting teens from welfare dependency to self-sufficiency, *Young Families Can*. She also received an award for "Women Who Make a Difference" from the Phoenix Women's Commission.

Ms. McClure served as Executive Officer for the California State Council on Mental Health. She organized the first state-wide Mental Health Consumer Conference and received commendation for Outstanding Contributions to Improving Mental Health Services in the State of California from the California State Assembly.

Ms. McClure's education includes a Masters Degree in Social Work from the University of Michigan, a Master of Science Degree in Public Health from Harvard University and a Bachelor of Science Degree in Sociology from Tuskegee University (formally Tuskegee Institute).

Ms. McClure's record of public service is consistent with her professional and educational experiences. She has served on the Sacramento County Mental Health Advisory Board, the board of the YWCA in Phoenix and Memphis and the board of the YMCA of Metro-Memphis. In 1995, Tennessee Governor McWherter appointed her to the Tennessee Commission on Children and Youth and she graduated from Leadership Memphis in 1996. Ms. McClure has provided leadership in many church and family programs and initiatives; however, she is most grateful for opportunities to mentor other women.

Ms. McClure's goal in every professional and volunteer endeavor is to improve the circumstances and outcomes for individuals and organizations. She is a change agent.

Her current journey includes the launching of a national empowerment movement targeting African-American women. She envisions a population of African-American women who display empowering attitudes and behaviors at every stage of life.

Ms. McClure believes that when women empower themselves to embrace and act on their greatness, they change the world one woman at a time, one family at a time and one community at a time.

Share the empowerment journey with others
Order additional copies of this journal

To order individual copies:

Go to Amazon.com

Bulk quantity purchases for educational, health promotion, fund-raisers, workforce development and service projects:

Visit www.ITSINMYHANDS.COM

Email: alnitapurpose08@Gmail.com

Or call: 1-800-424-2104

To request training material, motivational material, training and speaking engagements:

Visit www.ITSINMYHANDS.COM

Made in the USA
Charleston, SC
30 September 2010